Guide to

Western
Mushrooms

McLennan

By J.E. Underhill

Introduction

Mushrooms have attracted and intrigued mankind through the ages. Their sudden, ghostly appearance, the deadly qualities of some species and the hallucinogenic properties of others, contrasting so sharply with the delicious flavors that certain wholesome varieties bring to our tables, all lead us to view these strange plants with special curiosity and wonder.

Most people seem to want to know first if a strange mushroom is edible or dangerous. This small book is a guide to some of the most common mushrooms of the Pacific Northwest, and it identifies some of these as safe varieties for the beginner to eat. It also tries to go beyond that to generate awareness of the various vital roles the mushrooms play in the community of life and to spark an interest in their fascinating variations and adaptations.

The enjoyment of mushrooms doesn't start with the smell from a frying pan. It starts with a walk in the woods a week or two after the first heavy autumn rains. The leaves are turning, and the air is brisk. That heady air, the charm of the mushrooms in their natural setting, the annual remembrance of their interesting functions, bring as much enjoyment as the tasty treats that may emerge later from the kitchen.

The full story of the importance of mushrooms in the plant world is far from being understood today, and only a little of it can be stated here. The mushroom that you see is a 'fruiting body', roughly equivalent to the fruit of other plants. The vegetative part of the mushroom plant is a thready mass hidden within the material it feeds upon - a log, cow dung, buried wood, an insect pupa or whatever. Mushrooms do not contain or need green chlorophyll, the substance which, in higher plants, captures the energy of sunlight to create biological energy. Mushrooms, like all the great group of fungi to which they belong, get their energy second-hand.

Many form beneficial partnerships with the trees of our forests and are essential to their well-being. No mushroom is either good or bad in the natural community of life.

What Kind Is It?

Some mushrooms are easy to identify by sight, while others are so difficult that experts may disagree. Often it is necessary to make a spore print. To do this, put a fresh cap, gills or pores down, on a piece of white paper, then cover it with a bowl or glass. After an hour or two, there will usually be spore deposit with a definite color, even white shows. Many species require microscopic examination or chemical tests for positive identification. For the beginner these must remain simply unidentified plants of beauty and interest.

While close to seventy common species of mushrooms of the Pacific Northwest are listed here, there are hundreds of other varieties left out. That includes all of the myriad of tiny ones which, though lovely to see and photograph, are generally very difficult to identify. Don't try to force any mushroom to fit a description given here unless it clearly agrees with all points in both the test and the illustration.

In general the species are listed here in groups of similar spore color. A few exceptions have been made to bring look-alikes together.

All mushroom seekers should form the habit of making detailed field notes, as well as spore prints, of strange species. You will learn to see mushrooms more thoroughly this way, and you will be able to identify them later at home or in library reference books.

Beginners run the risk of confusing themselves if they try to learn too many mushrooms at once. Learn four or five kinds on each outing -- but learn them well.

The Goods and The Bads:

We recommend eating only twelve species. Why, when so many others are noted as being edible? Because these twelve are especially easy to recognize and cannot be readily confused with species that are dangerous. In addition, all twelve are choice and tasty if properly prepared. Experienced mushroom hunters do use other kinds, but they know how to distinguish a particular species from dangerous look-alikes. Most of the others listed here are of poorer quality, and some may be confused with toxic varieties. They are not the best for the beginner to experiment with. Many non-poisonous mushrooms are tough, stringy, bitter, or otherwise unpalatable.

Poisonous mushrooms differ in their effects according to the chemical nature of their toxins. Scientists recognize six or seven quite different classes of mushroom poisons. The most virulent, such as some *Amanita* species, are often deadly, and there are other toxins of equal potency. Some poisons cause varying degrees of illness but are not usually fatal. To complicate matters, there are mushrooms, such as *Gyromitra esculenta,* which are apparently fine edibles in parts of their ranges, yet very poisonous in other places. Also there are many mushrooms which some people can eat and enjoy but which make other people very ill. These last contain substances to which only the victims are sensitive. For many species, the question of edibility or toxicity has yet to be determined.

And In The Kitchen

Cut off stalk bases in the field and clean off excess dirt from caps before carrying mushrooms home. Use a basket to minimize crushing. Bring into the kitchen only carefully chosen, fresh, worm-free mushrooms of sure, safe identity. Keep the rest in another place.

Rinse each cap under cold water, checking for hidden insects. Slit morel mushrooms and check inside. Discard tough stalks and any diseased parts.

Generally, mushrooms may be fried in butter, sliced fresh into salads, simmered in soups, baked in casseroles, or added to sauces. Just how you use them is largely a matter of personal choice. Onion, garlic, sour cream, and certain spices - nutmeg is one - enhance the flavor of some species. The text provides suggestions for preparing particular kinds of mushrooms.

In eastern Europe many people cut up mushrooms and string the bits in a warm place where they will dry for winter use. This can improve the flavor. In North America, we tend to substitute the deepfreeze. Mushrooms freeze best if first fried in butter, just until steaming stops. At this point cool them and freeze in plastic bags. Some types are also suitable for pickling or bottling, though I think this detracts from the natural flavor.

Mushroom Forays:

In many communities there are natural history clubs that sponsor mushroom hunts. If you attend one, you may observe that it is typical for experts to refrain from identifying many mushrooms by sight. Experts know the wisdom of caution.

On these walks, and on your own expeditions, carry along a sketch pad and pencil, or water color paints, and try your hand at depicting mushrooms by these means. Mushrooms are also prime subjects for photography. For this you will need a camera with a macro lens, extension tubes, or a bellows unit, any of which will enable you to move in close to your subject. With most mushroom shapes there is a problem in obtaining a sufficient depth of focus. You may overcome this to some extent by using small "f" stops and long exposures with natural lighting, or by substituting a synchronized electronic flash as an artificial high-intensity light source. In either case, fairly high speed film provides an additional advantage. Carry a penlight as an aid to focusing in the often dim light of the forest.

Treat mushrooms with respect and you will find that getting to know them is a richly rewarding experience.

More To Read

If you are going to learn more about mushrooms, you will wish to buy one of the more complete reference books. Here are some of the best for Pacific Northwest readers:

A Field Guide to The Western Mushrooms, by Alexander H. Smith (Ann Arbor: Univ. of Michigan Press, 1975)

Fungi, Delight of Curiosity, by Harold J. Brodie (Toronto: Univ. of Toronto Press, 1978) A charming book, in which a warmly philosophical scientist views the world of fungi.

Guide to Common Mushrooms of British Columbia, by R.J. Bandoni and A.F. Szczawinski (B.C. Provincial Museum Handbook No. 24, 1976)

Mushrooms of North America, by Orson K. Miller, Jr. (New York: Dutton, 1978)

The Savory Wild Mushroom, by Margaret McKenny (Seattle: Univ. of Washington Press, 1971)

Acknowledgements

My thanks are extended to a number of people who have helped make this book possible. First to Dr. Adam Szczawinski who introduced me to mushrooms twenty years ago and, in his inimitable way, gave me an interest that has never flagged. Second to Dr. Al Funk who has more recently been my mushroom mentor, and who has kindly read this manuscript. Then I thank Jessie Woollett, Enid Lemon, Bill McLennan and Al Grass for making their fine photographs available, and Robert Sward and Dave Hancock for editorial guidance. Finally, I thank my wife, Elise, for her support and encouragement in this project.

Through the centuries from the time of Henry VIII to the American Civil War, mushrooms that caused dry rot plagued the oaken-hulled ships of Britain's Royal Navy. Ships needed constant repair and frequent replacement, and there were instances where rotted hulls collapsed at sea, drowning entire crews.

4

Spore print: white   Size: to about 30 cm width
Shape: egg-shaped in youth, becoming broadly convex in maturity
Texture: smooth, with few to many prominent, white, raised warts
Cap color: red to buff-yellow in different color forms
Flesh: moderately thick, white, and firm
Gills: free from the stalk, white, fine and crowded
Stalk: moderately thick, with a swollen base fitted into an obscurely cup-like 'volva',
           white, and bearing a ring

The even more poisonous *A. pantherina*, 'panther agaric,' has caps to 15 cm width, with a yellow to tan-brown color. Both species are common in partly shaded woodland edge throughout the warmer parts of the year. These *Amanitas* are probably responsible for most cases of mushroom poisoning in the Pacific Northwest. Learn to know them, for there are no rules of thumb that will tell you if a mushroom is edible or poisonous. The old 'silver spoon' and 'peeling' tests are meaningless.

One of the symptoms produced by *A. muscaria* is a state of berserk frenzy. Siberian peasants two centuries ago evidently enjoyed and sought this frenzy. They drank the urine of one of their number who had first eaten the mushroom and whose body evidently filtered out some of the more dangerous chemicals. Very old religious writings also suggest that this mushroom may have played a part in ancient religious rites. Despite these evidences of use, it is an extremely dangerous species to experiment with.

Amanita pantherina 'panther agaric'   McLennan

Amanita muscaria 'fly agaric'

Woollett

Spore print: pale ochre-yellow   Size: to 10 cm or more width
Shape: convex in youth, becoming irregularly vase-shaped
Texture: smooth and slightly moist
Cap color: soft egg-yolk orange
Flesh: thick, firm and with an odor of apricot
Gills: extending far down the stalk, very thick, forked, not crowded, and colored as the cap
Stalk: stout, often contorted, smooth, and colored as the cap

C. subalbidus 'white chanterelle' (also recommended) has a white spore print, is somewhat larger, and is cream-white in color. Otherwise it is similar to *C. cibarius.* Both species are fairly common in early autumn, often growing in colonies in association with Douglas fir and salal.

Both are edible and tasty, but beware of confusing *C. cibarius* with *Clitocybe aurantiaca,* which may be poisonous. Compare its description on the facing page.

Pick *Chanterelles* early in the season when they are firm. Cut them up, stems and all, then cook them slowly in butter until they just start to brown. Season with a dash of nutmeg and serve with turkey or pork. Cooked, they freeze well.

C. cibarius is the treasured 'pfefferling' of Germany. You may buy it as an expensive import in delicatessens - or gather your own for nothing!

Squirrels harvest summer mushroom caps, drying them on sunny stumps or tree boughs for later storage. They can evidently eat some kinds that are toxic to us.

Cantharellus sub-albidus 'white chanterelle'   JEU

Cantharellus cibarius 'chanterelle'

Woollett

Hypomyces has no real cap or gills or stalk. Rather, it is a fungus parasite of some *Russula* and *Lactarius* species, and possibly others. Its many minute orange fruiting bodies cover the host mushroom, hiding the original color, while the thready mycelium growing within the host distorts its shape to a vase-like form with coarse or absent gills. There is a possibility that the resulting growth could be mistaken for a chanterelle.

Hypomyces is common, so it is included here. There is also a green kind of *Hypomyces,* and some mushrooms are attacked by still other fungi. Infected mushrooms should not be eaten because it is usually impossible to determine the original species.

Clitocybe aurantiaca 'orange clitocybe'   POISONOUS

Spore print: white   Size: to about 8 cm width
Shape: first convex, becoming irregularly vase-like in age
Texture: smooth, velvety, and dry
Cap color: soft salmon-orange
Flesh: thin, soft, and pale orange
Gills: extending well down the stalk, thin, and more brightly colored than the cap
Stalk: slender, expanding downward, colored as the cap, lacking a ring, and often
        stained brown near the base

This is a common forest mushroom of early autumn. Its smaller size, thin gills and flesh easily distinguish it from *Cantharellus cibarius,* but compare the two. The toxicity of this species is not well established.

Hypomyces lactifluorum *with Chantarelle*

JEU

Clitocybe aurantiaca   'orange clitocybe'

Woollett

7

Hygrophorus   'waxy-cap hygrophorus'

Spore print: white   Size: to about 10 cm width
Shape: narrowly conical in youth, becoming broader with a central knob
Texture: smooth, shiny, and a little sticky
Cap color: bright orange to red
Flesh: orange-red and bruising black
Gills: attached to the stalk, yellowish, coarse, and with a distinctly waxy feel when
         rubbed between the fingers
Stalk: slender, hollow, lacking a ring, and colored like the cap

    Hygrophorus grows alone or in small colonies on the forest floor in the fall.
There are a number of varieties, most of them colorful and good subjects for the
camera. All have similar waxy gills. They are neither good to eat nor poisonous.

Hygrophorus eburneus   'ivory-cap hygrophorus'

Spore print: white   Size: to about 10 cm width
Shape: at first convex, becoming flattish, often with a central knob
Texture: smooth and slightly sticky
Cap color: glistening white to pale cream
Flesh: white and fairly thick
Gills: extending slightly down the stalk, waxy to the touch, white, coarse, and not
         crowded
Stalk: white, tapering downwards, and lacking a ring

    This is a fairly common mushroom in our conifer forests in mid-autumn. Its
edibility has not been established.

JEU

Hygrophorus conicus   'waxy-cap hygrophorus'

Hygrophorus eburneus   'ivory-cap hygrophorus'

Woollett

8

Laccaria laccata   'common laccaria'

Spore print: white   Size: to about 8 cm width
Shape: convex in youth, becoming dished with convoluted and upturned edges in age
Texture: rough and dry
Cap color: variably soft burnt-orange
Flesh: thin, and colored as the cap
Gills: partly attached to the stalk, coarse, thick, widely spaced and waxy
Stalk: slender, tall, fibrous, lacking a ring, and with a rough surface

Laccaria amethystina, 'purple laccaria,' is very similar apart from its smoky-violet color. Both species are common, often forming considerable colonies in forest glades or along woodland roads. Both are tough, tasteless, and unfit for eating.

"Mushroom" is the name we apply to those fungi with large fleshy fruiting bodies of a variety of shapes. The world teems with other fungi, many of which affect our lives directly. Bread molds, wheat rust, rose mildew, ringworm, and the yeasts are familiar examples. There are many thousands of others, most too small for the unaided eye to see, but present in vast numbers. Each plays its part in the complex web of life. Many are re-cyclers of dead tissues, while others prey upon living things and help regulate populations of plants and animals.

Laccaria laccata 'common laccaria'

McLennan

Laccaria amethystina 'purple laccaria'

JEU

9

Lactarius deliciosus   'delicious lactarius'

Spore print: pale buff-yellow   Size: to about 13 cm width
Shape: convex in youth, some becoming shallowly vase-like in age
Texture: almost smooth
Cap color: carrot orange with obscure concentric darker rings
Flesh: fairly thick, firm, brittle, yellowish, and bleeding an orange 'latex' when broken
Gills: attached to the stalk, fine, crowded
Stalk: stout, scarcely tapering, lacking a ring, and paler than the cap

     L. sanguifluus looks very similar, but is darker and has red latex. Both species are common, but usually solitary, in Douglas fir forests in mid-autumn. Both are fine edibles, but not on our recommended list, as some very similar *Lactarii* are dangerous. Do not experiment with this group without the help of an experienced mushroomer.

Lactarius aurantiacus   'orange lactarius'

Spore print: whitish   Size: to about 12 cm width
Shape: at first convex, becoming concave and irregular
Texture: smooth, and somewhat sticky when wet
Cap color: bright brick-orange
Flesh: paler than the cap, thin, and with a bitter taste
Gills: attached and running slightly down the stalk, fine, pale buff-orange, and exuding a white latex if cut. This latex does not change color
Stalk: slender, paler than the cap, and lacking a ring

     Lactarius rufus answers a very similar description, but has darker reddish caps and an intensely hot taste. Both species are common in mid-autumn in our conifer forests. Neither should be eaten.

     The *Lactarii* are thought to be 'mycorrhizal partners' of the big conifer trees. The hidden thready underground mycelia of the mushrooms associate with the roots of the trees and apparently pass essential minerals to the conifers while receiving needed moisture. Neither partner can thrive without the other.

Lactarius deliciosus   'delicious lactarius'

JEU

Lactarius aurantiacus
'orange lactarius'
JEU

Lepiota naucina 'white lepiota'

(Leucoagaricus naucina)

Spore print: white   Size: to about 11 cm width
Shape: egg-shaped at first, becoming convex to almost flat
Texture: usually smooth and dry
Cap color: usually clean white, sometimes faintly gray
Flesh: fairly thick, firm, and white
Gills: free from the stalk, white, crowded, and darkening to pinkish brown in age
Stalk: fairly slender, lacking a 'volva,' white, having a stem ring, and often having a
slightly swollen base

This is a mushroom of lawns and other grassy places in very early autumn. It is edible for some people but makes others ill, so it is best left alone by all. Also, it closely resembles deadly poisonous white *Amanita* species which, however, have a cup or 'volva' at the stem base.

Lepiota rachodes 'shaggy lepiota'

Spore print: white   Size: to about 23 cm width
Shape: almost globular in youth, becoming convex
Texture: dry and coarsely scaly
Cap color: brown-gray in youth, becoming whitish, mottled with many brown, curly,
coarse scales
Flesh: white, bruising orange-yellow, the marks darkening to red-brown
Gills: free from the stalk, crowded, white, and bruising orange-yellow
Stalk: rather tall, with a prominent ring near the top, enlarged toward the base,
smooth, and white

This is a fairly common autumn mushroom which appears around compost heaps and by rotting trees. It is edible and good, but does not rate a recommendation because of its similarity to *Lepiota molybdites,* which has a green spore print and is poisonous.

Lepiota rachodes 'shaggy lepiota'

Lepiota naucina
'white lepiota'
McLennan

E.K. Lemon

Marasmius oreades   'fairy ring mushroom'

Spore print: white   Size: to about 5 cm width
Shape: bell-shaped in youth, becoming flattish with a central knob in age
Texture: smooth and dry
Cap color: soft reddish-brown to pale buff
Flesh: thin and pale
Gills: barely attached to the stalk, paler than the cap, and not crowded
Stalk: slender, fibrous, tough, lacking a ring, and darkest toward the base

This is the common 'fairy-ring' that damages many lawns. A ring colony may appear for many years, widening annually. *M. oreades* is edible and tasty, but people trying it for the first time should have someone experienced check what they collect. There are fairly similar but very poisonous brown mushrooms that occur on lawns.

Some forest mushrooms, such as *Hydnum repandum,* may also develop ring colonies.

Armillaria mellea   'honey mushroom'

(Armillariella mellea)

Spore print: white   Size: to about 11 cm width
Shape: convex in youth, becoming flattish with a central knob
Texture: smooth near the edges, but hairy-scaly toward the center
Cap color: honey-brown to dark brown
Flesh: thin and pale brown
Gills: attached to the stalk, extending a little downwards, and cream in color
Stalk: variable, but with a prominent ring near the top, and often swollen and flushed
          yellow near the base (many stalks often arise from one common base)

Armillaria mellea feeds upon living or dead plant tissues of many kinds. It is often of considerable concern to foresters when it attacks saleable timber.

Honey mushroom is delicious fried in butter with a little onion or garlic, and is highly valued in eastern Europe. Unfortunately, it is very variable and possible to confuse with other quite dangerous mushrooms, so it cannot be recommended for beginners.

Armillaria mellea 'honey mushroom'   JEU   **Marasmius oreades** 'fairy ring mushroom'

McLennan

12

Armillaria ponderosa   'pine mushroom'

Spore print: white   Size: to about 20 cm width
Shape: at first convex, becoming flattish in age
Texture: smooth at first, but developing a fine scaly surface
Cap color: white in youth, but developing fine brown scales that are densest near the center
Flesh: thick, white, firm, and with a sweet, aromatic odor
Gills: notched where they join the stalk, fine, crowded, and white, darkening to brownish in age
Stalk: very stout, with a conspicuous flaring ring, and tapering downwards below the ring

This is a widespread edible mushroom in conifer forests of the Pacific Northwest, though its abundance varies greatly from year to year. The Japanese people, who especially seek it, call it 'matsutake.'

Russula brevipes   'short-stemmed russula'

Spore print: creamy-white   Size: to over 20 cm width
Shape: at first convex, then becoming broadly concave
Texture: dry and almost smooth
Cap color: dingy white, often with brown bruise stains
Flesh: fairly thick, firm, white, and with a rather hot taste
Gills: extending slightly down the stalk to an abrupt termination, white, close, and thin
Stalk: very stout and short, white, lacking a ring, and bruising brown

Many *Russula* species occur in the Northwest. All are brittle, many are brightly colored, and as a group they resemble the *Lactarii,* but without the latex. There are many look-alikes, so field identification may be very difficult. Most are non-poisonous, at least one is possibly poisonous, and none are on our recommended list.

Armillaria ponderosa   'pine mushroom'

Russula brevipes   'short-stemmed russula'

Woollett   McLennan

Russula emetica 'emetic russula'   POISONOUS

Spore print: white   Size: to about 12 cm broad
Shape: convex in youth, becoming slightly concave in age
Texture: smooth, and slightly sticky
Cap color: bright red, fading as the cap ages
Flesh: thin, brittle, white, but pink just beneath the skin, and with a peppery, acrid
        taste
Gills: barely reaching the stalk, white, crowded and forked
Stalk: fairly stout, pure white, and lacking a ring

This is a fairly common solitary or colonial mushroom of coastal conifer forests in early autumn. As the name suggests, there is evidence that it is somewhat poisonous, though not all authorities agree.

There are so many variations of the reddish *Russula* species that even experienced mushroomers are sometimes puzzled by them.

Russula xerampelina 'woodland russula'

Spore print: pale yellow   Size: to about 17 cm width
Shape: convex in youth, becoming shallowly dished
Texture: smooth; sticky when wet
Cap color: usually purplish-red with brown or olive flushing, but there are several color
           variations
Flesh: thin, firm, brittle, white, and with a pronounced fishy odor
Gills: notched against the stalk, pale buff yellow, crowded, and bruising brownish-
        orange
Stalk: stout, scarcely tapered, lacking a ring, and white with pink suffusion

This is another very common mushroom of our conifer forests in autumn. Despite its fishy odor some people enjoy eating it, but it is not recommended.

Pleurotus ostreatus 'oyster mushroom'   RECOMMENDED

Spore print: lilac   Size: to about 25 cm width
Shape: caps are off-center, with the attachment or short stalk at the margin. The top is
        irregularly convex
Texture: smooth
Cap color: whitish to yellow-brown, but not orange
Flesh: fairly thick and whitish
Gills: extending down the short stalk, white or buff, coarse and not crowded

P. ostreatus generally is found in colonies on damp, rotting hardwoods and occurs in both spring and early autumn. The very similar *P. sapidus* has white spores and is similarly edible. *P. porrigens,* the 'angel wings,' is smaller, always white, has thin, crowded gills and thin flesh. It is edible, but inferior, and grows on rotting conifers.

All of these mushrooms should be picked very young for eating, for they are soon attacked by tiny beetle larvae.

Many mushrooms attract particular species of small flies or beetles that lay their eggs in the gills, pores, or stalks. The eggs hatch rapidly into small grubs or 'worms' that tunnel and feed within the mushroom. When fully fed, they pupate underground, later hatching as adults to complete their cycle.

Russula emetica 'emetic russula'

Russula xerampelina 'woodlands russula'

McLennan

Pleurotus porrigens 'angel wings'

Woollett

Pleurotus ostreatus 'oyster mushroom'

Woollett

15

Tricholoma personatum 'blewit'

(Lepista nuda = Clitocybe nuda)

Spore print: pale buff-pink   Size: to about 14 cm width
Shape: convex in youth, becoming flattish with a slight knob
Texture: smooth and dry
Cap color: gray-brown with a lilac suffusion, but variable and fading to pale buff
Flesh: moderately thick, tinged lavender, and with a fragrant odor
Gills: notched against the stalk, pale blue-lavender, becoming lilac-buff, and crowded
Stalk: fairly stout, often bulbous at the base, pale violet to whitish, and lacking a ring

Blewits are fairly common mushrooms of autumn in our forests. They are good edibles, but learners need the help of someone experienced because there is the danger of confusion with other species.

Cortinarius alboviolaceus 'silvery cortinarius'

Spore print: rusty brown   Size: to about 7 cm in width
Shape: bell-shaped in youth, becoming flat and knobbed in age
Texture: silvery, silky and dry
Cap color: silvery light violet
Flesh: thin, firm, and tinted violet
Gills: attached to the stalk, violet, aging to cinnamon-brown, thin and crowded, hidden by a cobwebby veil in youth
Stalk: moderately thick, enlarged toward the base, colored as the cap, and later may carry cobwebby remnants of the veil

This mushroom is found alone or in small colonies on the forest floor in autumn. *Cortinarius* has several hundred species, most of them believed to be mycorrhizal partners of the forest trees. Typically they are recognizable by the cobwebby veil and the rusty spore print. The edibility of most of them is unknown, and they should not be eaten.

Cortinarius alboviolaceus 'silvery cortinarius'

Tricholoma personatum 'blewit'   Woollett

JEU

Cortinarius cinnamomeus 'cinnamon cortinarius'

Spore print: rusty-brown   Size: to about 7 cm width
Shape: deeply convex in youth, becoming almost flat in age
Texture: almost smooth, with some shiny hairiness
Cap color: variably yellow-brown to warm-brown
Flesh: thin and yellowish
Gills: barely attached to the stalk, yellowish, becoming cinnamon-brown, fine and crowded, with the typical cobwebby veil in youth
Stalk: moderately stout, scarcely tapering, yellow-buff, and later with cobwebby remnants of the veil

    This species is found singly or in small groups in our coniferous forests in autumn. Its edibility has not been established.

Hebeloma crustiliniforme 'poison pie'   POISONOUS

Spore print: variably yellow-brown   Size: to about 8 cm width
Shape: convex in youth, becoming almost flat in age
Texture: smooth and slightly sticky
Cap color: light yellow-brown, paling to cream at the edges
Flesh: thick, white to yellow-brown, and with an odor of radishes
Gills: notched at the stalk, whitish, becoming smoky-gray-brown, and crowded
Stalk: fairly stout, may have an enlarged base, finely hairy, and lacking a ring

    This very poisonous mushroom grows alone or in small groups on the forest floor in autumn. Its mature gill color somewhat resembles that of some *Agaricus* species, but these have stalks with rings.

    If you really want to see mushrooms, try painting some of the kinds you find. Water colors are ideal for reproducing the subtle gradations of color.

Hebeloma crustiliniforme 'poison pie'   *JEU*

Cortinarius cinnamoneus 'cinnamon cortinarius'

Agaricus augustus 'the prince'

Spore print: purplish-brown   Size: to about 30 cm width
Shape: rounded with a flat top in youth, becoming broadly convex
Texture: finely scaly and dry
Cap color: variably whitish to pale tan with numerous brown scales in obscurely con-
centric rings, and bruising yellow
Flesh: thick, whitish, bruising yellow, and with an almond odor
Gills: free from the stalk, pale pink, aging to brown, and crowded
Stalk: stout and short, white but aging brown, with a heavy ring near the top in youth,
and scaly below the ring

This species is one of our choicest edible mushrooms. It is widespread, but not
abundant on open ground. A big cap of *A. augustus* sliced and fried in butter and served with beef is food for a king. Spore color and gill color readily separate it from
Lepiota rachodes, and there are other differences.

Agaricus campestris 'meadow mushroom'

Spore print: chocolate-brown   Size: to about 11 cm width
Shape: almost spherical in youth, becoming convex then almost flat
Texture: dry and almost smooth
Cap color: white when young, browning in age
Flesh: thick, firm, and with the 'traditional' mushroom odor
Gills: free from the stalk, pale pink darkening in age to brown, and fine
Stalk: stout, whitish, smooth, with a thin ring near the top, and not staining when
bruised

This is the common meadow mushroom of lawns and pastures, and is closely
related to the kind sold in stores. It does not grow in the forest. We especially like this
species sliced, uncooked, in a salad.

Agaricus arvensis, the 'horse mushroom' looks similar but grows larger,
bruises yellow, and has an odor of licorice. It, too, is good to eat.

Agaricus placomyces has a smoky gray-brown cap, stains yellow, and often
smells of carbolic acid. It makes some people quite ill, so it should be avoided.

Agaricus agustus 'the prince'

McLellan

Mushroom spores are far tinier than the seeds of higher plants, so that the wind may bear them great distances. Mushroom species are thus apt to be widely distributed unless they have special growth requirements. Some, for example, will only grow on the tissues of a particular plant, so cannot spread beyond its range.

Agaricus campestris 'meadow mushroom'

JEU

Agaricus placomyces

Pholiota squarrosa adiposa 'fat pholiota'

Spore print: brown   Size: to about 10 cm width
Shape: almost globular in youth, becoming convex at maturity
Texture: scaly and dry in youth, sticky at maturity
Cap color: pallid yellow with abundant dark brown curly scales
Flesh: yellow
Gills: attached to the stalk or notched, pale yellow at first, darkening with age
Stalk: moderately stout, bearing a ring, below which it is scaly and darker. This spe-
         cies produces several stalks from a common base

    Fat pholiota occurs on logs or stumps of decaying hardwoods, especially maple, and produces large colorful colonies in early autumn. There are closely related and similar varieties that grow   upon other kinds of wood. None are recommended for eating.

Naematoloma fasciculare 'sulfur top'   POISONOUS

Spore print: purple-brown   Size: to about 7 cm width
Shape: rounded in youth, becoming convex, then almost flat
Texture: smooth
Cap color: bright yellow with a greenish cast
Flesh: thin, yellow, bruising brown, and very bitter
Gills: attached to the stalk in youth, yellow, becoming yellow-green at maturity, thin
         and crowded
Stalk: slender, hollow, smooth, buff to brown, bearing little sign of a ring, and
         generally many from a common base

    This is another common early autumn mushroom found on hardwood logs in dense clusters. Sometimes, too, it attacks living trees. The intensely bitter flavor would deter most people from eating it, but there have been reports of poisonings as well. Don't try it.

    This is a good species in which to observe the thready mycelium or 'vegetable' substance from which a mushroom arises. Pull back a little of the moss or bark through which the cluster springs and have a look.

Pholiota squarrosa adiposa 'fat pholiota'

Naematoloma fasciculare 'sulfur top'   JEU

JEU

20

Stropharia ambigua 'questionable stropharia'

Spore print: purple-brown   Size: to about 10 cm width
Shape: convex in youth, becoming flat and broadly knobbed in age
Texture: smooth and sticky, with conspicuous particles of veil hanging from the cap margin
Cap color: ochre-yellow with white veil particles
Flesh: thin and whitish
Gills: attached to the stalk, whitish but darkening gray-purple with age, and not crowded
Stalk: slender, fairly tall, thickening toward the base, bearing a ring, and white-scaly below the ring

   This is a common, usually solitary, mushroom of the Northwest coniferous forests in mid-autumn. It is neither edible nor poisonous.

   Though this species is not hallucinogenic, it is related to a considerable number that are. People who experiment with hallucinogenic mushrooms are extremely foolish, as some of the species involved are very easily confused in the field and the poisons which they contain can be severe or deadly.

Gomphidius subroseus 'rosy gomphidius'

Spore print: dark smoky-gray   Size: to about 8 cm width
Shape: rounded in youth, becoming broadly convex in age
Texture: shiny, with a peelable layer of clear slime
Cap color: soft smoky-rose
Flesh: fairly thick, whitish, and soft
Gills: extending down the stalk a short distance, whitish becoming gray, and fairly crowded
Stalk: fairly stout, scarcely tapering, bearing an evident ring of dark hairs just beneath the cap, and often flushed yellow near the base

   G. glutinosus, 'peg-top gomphidius' has the same general description, but with a grayish purple-brown cap. All its parts bruise black. Both species are quite common in our forests in mid-autumn. Both are edible, but not of good quality.

Gomphidius subroseus 'rosy gomphidius'   Woollett

A. Grass

Stropharia ambigua 'questionable stropharia'

21

Coprinus comatus 'shaggy mane'

Spore print: black   Size: to about 11 cm height
Shape: narrowly egg-shaped in youth, then almost cylindrical, becoming conical in age
Texture: rough with soft, shaggy scales
Cap color: usually white, but scales may be tipped with tan
Flesh: thin, brittle and whitish, soon darkening to pink then black as the cap digests itself
Gills: free from the stalk, changing from white through pink to black as the cap 'auto-digests'
Stalk: moderately thick, hollow, brittle, white, and bearing a ring

Probably everyone knows the 'shaggy mane' that is so common on our lawns and roadsides in late summer and autumn. It often occurs in dense clusters. No other mushroom is so easy to find or identify, or as safe to eat.

Pick 'shaggy manes' before they show any black. We like them cooked very promptly, for they will not keep at all. We fry them in butter until they just begin to toast brown, and we add a touch of sour cream at the last. We serve them on toast beside chicken or other delicate food.

Coprinus atramentarius 'inky cap'

Spore print: black   Size: to about 8 cm in height
Shape: egg-shaped in youth, becoming bell-shaped or conical in maturity
Texture: almost smooth or with fine vertical lining
Cap color: silvery dove-gray, soon blackening from below
Flesh: thin and colored as the cap
Gills: free from the stalk, pale gray but soon blackening and 'auto-digesting' to a black liquid
Stalk: slender, scarcely tapering, hollow, pale, with a ring low down, often many from a common base

Inky caps often occur in tight clusters on lawns or roadsides, probably feeding upon buried wood. They are edible and safe to eat when young, but may produce violent flushing, palpitations, and heat sensations if consumed within twenty-four hours before or after use of alcoholic beverages.

Coprinus comatus 'shaggy mane'

Coprinus atramentarius 'inky cap'

Woollett

22

Coprinus micaceus 'shiny cap'

Spore print: black-brown   Size: to about 3 cm width
Shape: bell-shaped with conspicuous vertical grooving
Texture: dry and smooth, with a dusting of shining whitish particles when young
Cap color: ochre-brown
Flesh: thin and pale brown
Gills: notched at the stalk, crowded, pallid, turn brown in age, and do not become
         inky like other members of this group
Stalk: thin, hollow, whitish, and many from a common base

   C. micaceus grows in both spring and autumn at the base of old stumps or on other rotting wood. Like others of its group, it is edible, but beginners will do well to check it out with someone experienced, for there are many other little brown mushrooms that may be dangerous to some degree.

Boletinus lakei 'lake's boletinus'

(Suillus lakei)

Spore print: olive-yellow   Size: to about 17 cm width
Shape: convex in youth, flattening in maturity
Texture: softly rough-scaly
Cap color: appears orange-brown with numerous small brown scales on a yellowish
           background
Flesh: yellow, and does not change color when bruised
Pores (not gills): pore mouths bright yellow, bruising brown, and arranged more or less
           radially; pore layer does not readily separate from the cap
Stalk: yellow, streaked brown, slightly scaly, and bearing a faint ring

   Lake's boletinus is very common in the forest floor 'duff' of our Douglas fir forests. It appears over a long period, starting in late summer. This, like most members of the pore-bearing Boletus family, is edible but inferior. The general rule is that members of this group are safe to eat if the pore mouths are not red and if the caps do not turn blue immediately when cut. Most boletes are best left as handsome decorations for the forest, despite the fact that they are much sought after as food in eastern Europe.

Coprinus micaceus 'shiny cap'

Boletinus lakei 'lake's boletinus'

JEU

23

Boletus edulis 'king boletus'

Spore print: olive-brown   Size: to over 25 cm width
Shape: convex in youth, becoming broadly convex in age
Texture: smooth and dry
Cap color: variably tan to mid-brown and even over cap
Flesh: very thick, firm, white, and does not change color
Pores: pore mouths whitish, darkening to buff
Stalk: very stout and often much enlarged at the base, whitish, aging to buff, and
      with a finely netted surface

      This is probably the best of our edible boletes, useful in soups, sauces and simply fried. In Europe, where it is much prized, it is often cut up then dried carefully for storage. Watch for it in open woodlands and glades.

Boletus mirabilis 'admirable boletus'

Spore print: dark olive-brown   Size: to about 16 cm width
Shape: convex in youth, broadening in age
Texture: roughly hairy-scaly
Cap color: variably a dark red-brown
Flesh: thick, pale yellow but flushed red just beneath the skin, and not bruising blue
Pores: pore mouths bright yellow, aging to mustard
Stalk: yellow, streaked with red-brown, and often with a rough texture

      Admirable boletus is often found growing alone or in small groups on rotting wood, usually hemlock, in mid-autumn. It is edible, and it is not as subject to insect attack as some other boletes, but I think it a better subject for a painting or a photograph than for the frying pan.

      Boletus zelleri answers a rather similar description, but its cap has a velvety, heavily-powdered appearance, and its flesh sometimes slowly stains blue.

      Break off a piece of the cap of a strange mushroom to look for signs of white or colored latex (*Lactarius* species) and to observe if the latex changes color. Also watch for discolorations from bruising. Both signs are important for identification and should go into field notes.

Boletus edulis 'king boletus'

McLennan

Boletus mirabilis
'admirable boletus'

Clavaria spp. 'coral fungi'

The many *Clavarias* vie with the bright leaves of October in decorating the forest floor, but refuse to take second place with their strange and beautiful array of shapes. Most are coral-like, but others are finger or club-shaped, and they present a handsome variety of colors. In general they are hard to identify, but this in no way lessens their value as subjects for the camera, the brush, or the eye of the autumn stroller.

Clavaria flava 'coral fungi'

JEU

Clavaria delphus truncatus

Ramaria subbotrytis

McLennan   Parks Brd.

JEU

Clavaria cristata

25

Aleuria aurantia 'orange fairy-cup'

Along woodland road edges, after early autumn rains, these bright and attractive fungi often cluster in the hard ground in great numbers. Individual cups measure to perhaps 8 cm across, slowly flattening, and often becoming wavy and twisted.

Where the cap fungi shelter their spores beneath a protective cap and let them drift from the gills or pores onto the breeze, the fairy-cups have a different scheme. They puff out their spores in little clouds. You may prompt one to do this if you scrunch low on your knees and blow a short sharp puff at it. If conditions are right, it will promptly puff up a little cloud right back at you.

There is a variety of related fairy cups in yellows, reds, and brown.

Dacrymyces palmatus 'witches' butter'
Tremella mesenterica

These two quite similar fungi are common on stumps and logs in the Pacific Northwest in the damp weather of autumn. Both form small to medium masses of yellow to orange, convoluted 'brain-like' shapes with a consistency like jelly.

The dried 'cloud ears' sold in Chinese food stores are a related mushroom, shipped in from the Orient.

Hydnum repandum 'hedgehog mushroom'   RECOMMENDED
(Dentinum repandum)

Spore print: white   Size: to about 10 cm width, but very variable
Shape: rounded in youth, becoming irregularly convex in age
Texture: dry and smooth-of slightly scaly
Cap color: light orange-brown, and variable
Flesh: thick, brittle, soft, and almost white
Teeth (not gills): extending slightly down the stalk, uneven in length, paler than the cap, and very fragile
Stalk: fairly stout, often distorted, pale, brittle, and smooth

This is a very late autumn mushroom, usually occuring in November or later in the forest and often found in 'fairy rings.' The whole mushroom, including stalk, is a choice tidbit for your table. This is a species that is almost never attacked by insects. It has a delicate nutty, cheesy taste that is quite different from that of other mushrooms. We fry it in butter and serve it on points of toast.

Polyporus sulfureus 'sulfur polypore'

This common 'shelf fungus' needs no more description than the picture gives, for there is nothing else like it in our area. Individual lobes may reach over 40 cm in width. Their bottom surfaces bear fine pores from which the almost microscopic spores are released. The tender edges of sulfur polypore are edible and fairly good when the growth is young.

The polypores are a very common group of mushrooms in our forests. Many people are familiar with the 'shelves' or 'brackets' that grow from stumps and forest trees. Some of these feed upon dead wood, but others attack and may severely damage living trees. As a group, therefore, the polypores are of special concern to foresters.

Aleuria aurantia orange fairy-cup'

Tremella mesenterica

Woollett

Dacrymyces palmatus 'witches butter'

A. Grass

Hydnum repandum 'hedgehog mushroom'

Polyporus sulfureus 'sulfur polypore'

McLennan

27

Even young specimens of this are 12 cm broad, and some will reach several times that size. They have a globular shape in maturity but are narrowed below when young. The outer rind in this species cracks into broad, shallow scales and is very white, slowly browning in age. The closely related *C. gigantea,* which is the giant puffball further east, is smooth but similar in other respects. Giant puffballs are best known in our area in moist pastures of the interior, where they occur in mid-summer.

All the **white-fleshed puffballs** are good eating, even the little *Lycoperdon perlatum,* though it is a fuss to prepare. Beware, though, for we have a yellow-brown puffball, *Scleroderma aurantium,* with **purplish-gray flesh** that has caused many cases of **poisoning. Be sure** what you harvest to eat is a puffball, and not an immature cap mushroom. Slice them down the middle to see.

Dip quarter-inch slices of snowy-white puffball into beaten egg, then cracker crumbs, before frying. A chicken will die happily if it can be served with fried puffball slices!

Sparassis radicata 'cauliflower fungus'

This is a spectacular fungus that may reach over 75 cm in diameter and may weigh 15 kg or more, but it varies greatly in size. Its form is best described by its name. (See picture.) The color is white or pale lemon-yellow, browning slowly in age. The fleshy, flattened branchlets are soft and flexible but grow tougher in time. 'Cauliflower fungus' is normally found alone and usually grows at the base of a coniferous tree.

This is an edible species, but in my opinion it is quite inferior. With the twelve RECOMMENDED kinds usually easy to find, why bother with less tasty fare?

Nidula candida 'bird's nest fungus'

Nearly everyone who walks a forest trail soon discovers this small fungus clinging to some fallen branch and marvels at its strange shape. As a rule they are found as colonies of little goblets, each smaller than the tip of your small finger. Each 'goblet' begins to form from the mycelium as a tiny puffball-like growth. Presently the top breaks off to reveal a cup holding a number of 'seed-like' packets of many minute spores. The cup is designed so that a rain drop hitting it will throw the spore packets as far as possible. Each packet is equipped with a long thready tail, and many catch on nearby leaves. Now nature requires that the packet be eaten, with the leaf, by a passing animal. Eventually the released spores fall to the ground some distance away in the animal's droppings and, if circumstances are right, a new cup-colony may form.

We think of mushrooms as plants, but are they really plants? They have no green chlorophyll with which to use sun energy to make food as other plants do. Like animals, they get all their sustenance from food already stored in living or dead tissues. Cell walls of mushrooms contain material like that of our fingernails - or an ant's body case. Some - the slime molds - can even travel about on rotting logs.

Calvatia booniana 'giant puffball'

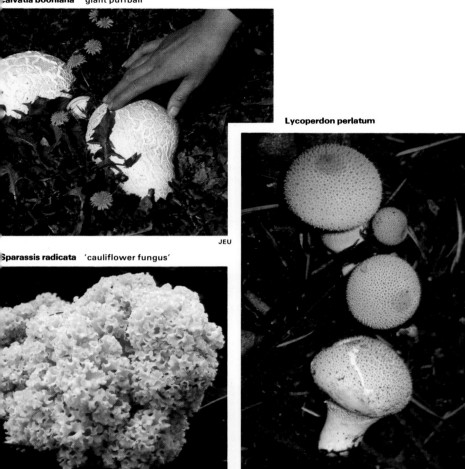

Lycoperdon perlatum

JEU

Sparassis radicata 'cauliflower fungus'

A. Grass   JEU

JEU

Nidula candida 'bird's nest fungus'

Gyromitra esculenta 'false morel' DANGEROUS

The appearance of this mushroom is, perhaps, most aptly described by its alternative common name 'brain mushroom.' Its **wrinkled and folded** cap may be as much as 10 cm broad, and varies from tan to dark brown, with a pallid stalk beneath.

This is a very puzzling mushroom, for though many people eat it with enjoyment, it has poisoned numerous others severely. Its effect evidently varies in different individuals, and its toxicity seems greater in some regions. Furthermore, there is a distinct risk of confusing it with related more poisonous species. Clearly **it is not a mushroom for beginners to eat.**

Compare the appearance of this mushroom carefully with that of the recommended *Morels.* See that *Gyromitra* is wrinkled and lobed, while *Morels* are pitted.

Helvella lacunosa 'elf's saddle'

Closely related to the *Gyromitras* are the *Helvellas.* This particular species is set apart by its ghostly whitish or gray or blackish cap set atop a beautifully sculptured stalk of usually paler hue. The cap is variously folded and wrinkled, with a frequent 'saddle' shape from which the common name derives. Watch for elf's saddle in open forests in early autumn. It occurs over a wide range.

With its infinitely varied forms, this is a marvelous mushroom to sketch or photograph. Don't pick it for food, however, as there are some rather similar mushrooms that are quite poisonous.

Helvella lacunosa 'elf's saddle' Woollett

Gyromitra esculenta 'false morel'

3

M. angusticeps has narrowly conical caps with distinct **pits separated by raised ridges** that are more or less vertically aligned. The cap **is attached at its base to the pale stalk.** In size the caps vary widely, but may sometimes exceed 10 cm in height. The color varies from a light gray-brown to a dark blackish-brown in age.

M. esculenta has a rounded tip to the cap, with the ridges usually more irregularly placed, and with a generally paler color. Otherwise the descriptions are the same, and the two kinds may be difficult for even experienced mushroomers to identify.

Both morels are found on fairly open ground in spring or early summer. They seem to prefer burned-over areas especially. Both are among the most delicious of mushrooms. They should be washed and slit open before cooking to rid them of hiding insects and, of course, wormy specimens should be discarded. They fry beautifully, but they may also be used in soups or stews.

Think of the problem our forests would soon have were it not for these mushrooms and other fungi and bacteria that ultimately return the substance of each log and twig and leaf to the soil and air from whence it came. Think about it!

Morchella angusticeps   'morel'

Morchella esculenta   'morel'

Index